To

_____

From

_____

Little Book

DEVOTIONS
31 DAILY DEVOTIONALS

Attitude

Little Book

DEVOTIONS

Attitude

The quoted ideas expressed in this book (but not scripture verses) are not, in all cases, exact quotations, as some have been edited for clarity and brevity. In all cases, the author has attempted to maintain the speaker's original intent. In some cases, quoted material for this book was obtained from secondary sources, primarily print media. While every effort was made to ensure the accuracy of these sources, the accuracy cannot be guaranteed. For additions, deletions, corrections or clarifications in future editions of this text, please write BRIGHTON BOOKS.

The Holy Bible, King James Version

The Holy Bible, New King James Version (NKJV) Copyright © 1982 by Thomas Nelson, Inc. Used by permission.

New Century Version®. (NCV) Copyright © 1987, 1988, 1991 by Word Publishing, a division of Thomas Nelson, Inc. All rights reserved. Used by permission.

International Children's Bible®, New Century Version®. (ICB) Copyright © 1986, 1988, 1999 by Tommy Nelson™, a division of Thomas Nelson, Inc. All rights reserved. Used by permission.

The Holman Christian Standard Bible™ (HCSB) Copyright © 1999, 2000, 2001 by Holman Bible Publishers. Used by permission.

The HOLY BIBLE, NEW INTERNATIONAL VERSION®. (NIV) Copyright © 1973, 1978, 1984 International Bible Society. Used by permission of Zondervan. All rights reserved.

The Holy Bible. New Living Translation (NLT) copyright © 1996 Tyndale Charitable Trust. Used by permission of Tyndale House Publishers.

Scripture taken from *The Message.* (MSG) Copyright © 1993, 1994, 1995, 1996, 2000, 2001, 2002. Used by permission of NavPress Publishing Group.

The prayers and essays in this book are written by Criswell Freeman; used with permission.

Compiled and Edited: Mary Susan Freeman
Cover Design: Kim Russell, Wahoo Designs
Page Layout: Bart Dawson

ISBN 1-58334-271-0

For All of God's Children

Table of Contents

A Message to Parents....................................13

1. Choosing the Right Attitude...................17
2. An Attitude That Makes God Smile.....21
3. Let's Celebrate!...25
4. When You Don't Feel Like
        Feeling Good....................................29
5. Let's Laugh!..33
6. Self-Control...37
7. An Attitude of Joy...................................41
8. A Peaceful Heart, A Peaceful Home....45
9. Looking at the Donut.............................49
10. An Attitude of Love..............................53
11. When You Need to Be Forgiven...........57
12. Solomon Says...61
13. Let's Be Thankful!..................................65
14. Blaming Others 69
15. You Can Do It . . .
        If You Stick to It!............................73
16. Telling the Truth....................................77
17. Respecting Other People.......................81

18. It Starts in the Heart..........................85

19. Watch What You Think.........................89

20. Words Are Important..........................93

21. Choosing Friends Wisely......................97

22. What the Bible Says...........................101

23. No More Tantrums.............................105

24. The Decision to Do What's Right.....109

25. Don't Be Too Hard on Yourself..........113

26. Count Your Blessings . . .
        and Keep Counting!............................117

27. Looking for the Good Things 121

28. Excuses, Excuses, Excuses 125

29. A Happy Heart . . . Day by Day.........129

30. Let's Praise God!.................................133

31. Jesus Loves Me, This I Know.............137

Bible Verses to Memorize.........................141

A Message to Parents

*C*ongratulations on picking up this book—it proves that you're vitally interested in the spiritual and intellectual development of your child.

This text is intended to be read by Christian parents to their young children. The book contains 31 brief chapters, one for each day of the month. Each chapter is composed of a Bible verse, a brief story, helpful hints for kids and for parents, and a prayer. Every chapter examines some aspect of an important Biblical theme: attitude.

For the next 31 days, try this experiment: read one chapter each night to your child, and then spend a few more moments talking about the chapter's meaning. By the end of the month, you will have had 31 different opportunities to share God's wisdom with your son or daughter, and that's good.

You know how God's love has transformed your own life. Now it's your turn to share that Good News with the boy or girl whom He has entrusted to your care. Happy reading! And may God continue to bless you and yours, now and forever.

Attitude

1

Choosing the Right Attitude

Your attitude should be the same that Christ Jesus had.

ତ୍ର ତ୍ର ତ୍ର

Philippians 2:5 NLT

Whats an attitude? The word *attitude* means "the way that you think." And don't forget this: your attitude is important.

Your attitude can make you happy or sad, grumpy or glad, joyful or mad. And, your attitude doesn't just control the way that you think; it also controls how you behave. If you have a good attitude, you'll behave well. And if you have a bad attitude, you're more likely to misbehave.

Have you spent anytime thinking about the way that you think? Do you pay much attention to your attitude? Hopefully so! After all, a good attitude is better than a bad one . . . lots better.

You have more control over your attitude than you think. So do your best to make your attitude a good attitude. One way you can do that is by learning about Jesus and about His attitude toward life. When you do, you'll learn that it's always better to think good thoughts, and it's always better to do good things.

Learn about Jesus and His attitude. Then try to do what Jesus would do.

WOW
Our attitude determines our approach to life.

John Maxwell

Parent Tip

Kids are amazingly intuitive: Believe it or not, your child is probably a mind reader. If your kid is like most kids, he or she is surprisingly sensitive. So do yourself and your child a favor: be careful with your thoughts as well as your actions.

Dear Lord,
I pray for an attitude that
pleases You. Even when I'm
angry, unhappy, tired, or upset,
I pray that I can remember what
it means to be a good person
and a good Christian.

Amen

An Attitude That Makes God Smile

Therefore, whether we are at home or away, we make it our aim to be pleasing to Him.

ฅ ฅ ฅ

2 Corinthians 5:9 HCSB

God knows everything about you, including your attitude. And when your attitude is good, God is pleased . . . very pleased.

Are you interested in pleasing God? Are you interested in pleasing your parents? Your teachers? And your friends? If so, try to make your attitude the best it can be. When you try hard to have a good attitude, you'll make other people feel better—and you'll make yourself feel better, too.

How can you please God? By having a good attitude, by obeying your parents and your teachers, and by being kind to your friends.

WOW

If you try to please God and God alone, you'll find yourself satisfied with life.

Kay Arthur

The importance of a parent's attitude: Parental attitudes are contagious. It's up to you to live your life—and treat your family—in a way that pleases God because He's watching carefully . . . and so, for that matter, are your kids.

Dear Lord,
thank You for all the blessings
You have given me. Today and
every day I will do my best to
please You by thinking good
thoughts and doing good deeds.

Amen

Let's Celebrate!

3

Rejoice in the Lord always.
I will say it again: Rejoice!

෨ ෨ ෨

Philippians 4:4 HCSB

Do you feel like celebrating today? Hopefully, you do feel like celebrating! After all, today (like every other day) should be a special time to thank God for all the wonderful things He has given you.

So don't wait for birthdays or holidays—make every day a special day, including this one. Take time to pause and thank God for His gifts. And then demonstrate your thanks by celebrating His world, His blessings, and His love.

Cheer up somebody else. Do you need a little cheering up? If so, find somebody else who needs cheering up, too. Then, do your best to brighten that person's day. When you do, you'll discover that cheering up other people is a wonderful way to cheer yourself up, too!

WOW
God is good, and heaven is forever.
Those two facts should brighten up
even the darkest day.
Marie T. Freeman

Cheerfulness is an attitude that is *highly contagious*: kids often catch it from their parents. Remember that cheerfulness starts at the top. A cheerful household usually begins with cheerful adults.

Dear Lord,
You have given me so many
reasons to be happy, and I want
to be a cheerful Christian.
Today and every day,
I will do my best to share
my happiness with my family
and my friends.

Amen

4
When You Don't Feel Like Feeling Good

We must not become tired of doing good.
We will receive our harvest of eternal life
at the right time. We must not give up!

🅢 🅢 🅢

Galatians 6:9 ICB

Where does a good attitude begin? It starts in our hearts and works its way out from there. Jesus taught us that a pure heart is a wonderful blessing. It's up to each of us to fill our hearts with love for God, love for Jesus, and love for all people. When we do, good things happen.

Sometimes, of course, we don't feel much like feeling good. Sometimes, when we're tired or frustrated or angry, we simply don't want to have a good attitude. On those days when we're feeling bad, it's time to calm down . . . and rest up.

Do you want to be the best person you can be? Then you shouldn't grow tired of doing the right things . . . and you shouldn't ever grow tired of thinking the right thoughts.

Want to feel better? Here are some things you can do: (1) Try not to misbehave. (2) Try to think good thoughts. (3) Try to cheer yourself up by cheering other people up. (4) Don't stay up late at night. And remember: if you're feeling really sick or really sad, tell your parents!

WOW
If you want to be truly happy,
be generous and kind.
Bill Hybels

Not feeling up to par? Try getting more sleep: If you're like most parents, you'll be tempted to get by on less sleep than you need. Don't do it. Make sure that you and your child go to bed early enough to get the sleep you need to feel good.

Dear Lord,
when I am feeling tired or sad,
I can always talk to You,
and I can always talk to my
parents, too. Thanks for
listening, Lord—and thank You
for parents who are willing to
listen and willing to help.

Amen

5
Let's Laugh!

There is a time for everything, and
everything on earth has its special season.
There is a time to cry and a time to laugh.
There is a time to be sad and
a time to dance.

🌀 🌀 🌀

Ecclesiastes 3:1, 4 NCV

Do you like to laugh? Of course you do! Laughter is a gift from God that He hopes you'll use in the right way. So here are a few things to remember:

1. God wants you to be happy.

2. Laughter is a good thing when you're laughing at the right things.

3. You should laugh with people, but you should never laugh at them.

God created laughter for a reason . . . and God knows best. So do yourself a favor: laugh at the right things . . . and laugh a lot!

Laughter is good medicine: So here's your prescription: Laugh lots!

WOW

There is nothing that lifts family spirits faster than when a lighthearted spirit fills the home and laughter fills its halls.

James Dobson

Parent Tip

Are we having fun yet? As a parent, it's up to you to make certain that your house is a place where everybody can expect to have good clean fun and plenty of laughs. How can you do so? By making certain that the good clean fun begins with you. Remember: if you're not having fun, neither, in all likelihood, are your kids.

Dear Lord,
laughter is Your gift.
Today and every day,
put a smile on my face,
and let me share that smile
with my friends and family . . .
especially my family.

Amen

Self-Control

6

So prepare your minds for service and have self-control. All your hope should be for the gift of grace that will be yours when Jesus Christ is shown to you.

ᔕ ᔕ ᔕ

1 Peter 1:13 NCV

Maybe you've heard the old proverb that says: "Look before you leap." What does that saying mean? It means that you should stop and think before you do something. Otherwise, you might be sorry you did it.

Learning how to control yourself is an important part of growing up. The more you learn about self-control, the better. Self-control will help you at home, at school, and at church. That's why parents and teachers are happy to talk about the rewards of good self-control. And that's why you should be excited about learning how important it is to look before you leap . . . not after!

Think first! Think before you say things . . . and think before you do things. Otherwise, you can get yourself in trouble. So here's a good rule to follow: Slow down long enough to think about the things you're about to do or say. That way, you'll make better choices.

WOW

No matter how many books you read, no matter how many schools you attend, you're never really wise until you start making wise choices.

Marie T. Freeman

Be an example of self-control: When it comes to parenting, you can't really teach it if you won't really live it.

Dear God,
today I will slow down and
think about things before
I do them. And when I slow down
to think about things,
I will always try to do
what's right.

Amen

An Attitude of Joy

Light shines on those who do right;
joy belongs to those who are honest.
Rejoice in the Lord, you who do right.
Praise his holy name.

৩ ৩ ৩

Psalm 97:11-12 NCV

God wants you to have a happy, joyful life. But that doesn't mean that you'll be happy all the time. Sometimes, you won't feel like feeling happy, and when you don't, your attitude won't be very good.

When you're feeling a little tired or sad, here's something to remember: This day is a gift from God. And it's up to you to enjoy this day by trying to be cheerful, helpful, courteous, and well-behaved. How can you do these things? A good place to start is by doing your best to think good thoughts.

Sometimes happy, sometimes sad: Even if you're a very good person, you won't be happy all the time. Sometimes, things will happen to make you sad, and it's okay to be sad when bad things happen to you, to your friends, or to your family. But remember: through good times and bad, God is always with you, and you are always protected.

WOW

Joy is a choice.
Joy is a matter of attitude that
stems from our faith in God.
Charles Swindoll

If you want to teach your child what it means to be a joyful Christian . . . be one.

Dear Lord,
You have given me so many
blessings, starting with
my family. I will keep joy in
my heart as I thank You, Lord,
for every single blessing
You've given me.

Amen

8

A Peaceful Heart, A Peaceful Home

I leave you peace; my peace I give you.
I do not give it to you as the world does.
So don't let your hearts be troubled
or afraid.

ک ک ک

John 14:27 NCV

Jesus offers us peace . . . peace in our hearts and peace in our homes. But He doesn't force us to enjoy His peace—we can either accept His peace or not.

When we accept the peace of Jesus Christ by opening up our hearts to Him, we feel much better about ourselves, our families, and our lives.

Would you like to feel a little better about yourself and a little better about your corner of the world? Then open up your heart to Jesus, because that's where real peace begins.

God's peace can be yours right now . . . if you open up your heart and invite Him in.

WOW
Peace with God is where all peace begins.
Jim Gallery

Peace at home . . . As the parent, you're in charge of keeping the peace and sharing it. It's a big job, so don't be afraid to ask for help . . . especially God's help.

Dear Lord,
I will open my heart to You.
And I thank You, God,
for Your love, for Your peace,
and for Your Son.

Amen

9
Looking at the Donut

You fill my cup to overflowing.
Surely your goodness and love will be
with me all my life, and I will live in
the house of the Lord forever.

🌀 🌀 🌀

Psalm 23:5-6 NCV

Here's a poem that was seen many years ago in a small donut shop:

As you travel through life brother,
Whatever be your goal,
Keep your eye upon the donut,
And not upon the hole.

What do you think these words mean? Well, this little poem can teach you an important lesson: You should spend more time looking at the things you have, not worrying about the things you don't have.

When you think about it, you've got more blessings than you can count. So make it a habit to thank God for the gifts He's given you, and don't feel jealous, angry, or sad about all the other stuff.

KiD TiP

Think about all the things you have (start-ing with your family and your faith) . . . and think about all the things you can do! If you think you can do something, you probably can. If you think you can't do some-thing, you probably can't. That's why it's so important to believe in yourself.

WOW

Optimism and cheerfulness are products of knowing Christ.

Billy Graham

Parent Tip

Be a living, breathing example of the power of optimism: Pessimism is contagious . . . make sure that your kids don't catch it from you.

51

Dear Lord,
I will look for the best
in other people, I will expect
the best from You, and I will try
my best to do my best—
today and every day.

Amen

10
An Attitude of Love

Dear friends, since God loved us
that much, we surely ought to
love each other.

🌀 🌀 🌀

1 John 4:11 NLT

Would you like to do something good today? If so, you can do it, and here's how: by obeying the Golden Rule.

Jesus told us that we should treat other people in the same way that we would want to be treated (that, of course, is the Golden Rule). But sometimes, especially when we're tired or upset, that rule is very hard to follow.

Jesus wants us to treat other people with respect, kindness, courtesy, and love. When we do, we make our families and friends happy . . . and we make our Father in heaven very proud.

So if you're wondering how to make the world a better place, here's a great place to start: let the Golden Rule be your rule, too. And if you want to know how to treat other people, ask the person you see every time you look into the mirror. The answer you receive will tell you exactly what to do.

Since you love them, say so! Since you sincerely love your family, make sure that you tell them so . . . a lot!

WOW
Kids go where there is excitement.
They stay where there is love.
Zig Ziglar

Be imaginative: There are so many ways to say "I love you." Find them. Put love notes in lunch pails and on pillows; hug relentlessly; laugh, play, and pray with abandon. Remember that love is highly contagious, and that your task, as a parent, is to ensure that your children catch it.

Dear Lord,
Your love is so wonderful that
I can't really imagine it,
but I can share it . . .
and I will . . . today
and every day.

Amen

11

When You Need to Be Forgiven

Stop judging others, and you will not be
judged. Stop criticizing others,
or it will all come back on you.
If you forgive others, you will be forgiven.

၆ ၆ ၆

Luke 6:37 NLT

Do you ever make mistakes? Of course you do! Even if you're a very good person, you're bound to make a mistake or two—everybody does.

When you do something you shouldn't have done, here are some things you can do:

1. Apologize to the people you've hurt, and ask for their forgiveness;
2. Fix the things you've messed up or broken;
3. Don't make the same mistake again;
4. Ask God for His forgiveness (which, by the way, He will give to you instantly);
5. Get busy doing something you can be proud of;
6. Don't be too hard on yourself . . . even if you made a mistake, you're still a very, very special person!

Forgive other people . . . and keep forgiving! Sometimes, you may forgive somebody once and then, in a little while, you may become angry at the very same person again. If so, you must forgive that person again and again . . . until it sticks!

WOW
Our forgiveness toward others
should flow from the fact that we know
God has forgiven us.
Franklin Graham

If it were easy, everybody would be doing it: Face facts: forgiveness can be a very hard thing to do. No matter. God instructs us to forgive others (and to keep forgiving them), period. As a parent, you must explain to your child that forgiving another person—even when it's difficult—is the right thing to do.

Dear Lord,
I have made mistakes,
and You have forgiven me.
Thank You for Your forgiveness.
When I am not perfect, help
other people to forgive me—
and help me forgive myself.

Amen

12

Solomon Says

You must choose for yourselves today
whom you will serve . . . as for me and
my family, we will serve the Lord.

෨ ෨ ෨

Joshua 24:15 NCV

Solomon was a king, a very wise man, and a very good writer. He even wrote several books in the Bible! So when He finally put down His pen, what was this wise man's final advice? It's simple; Solomon said: "Honor God and obey His commandments."

The next time you have an important choice to make, ask yourself this: "Am I honoring God and obeying Him? And am I doing what God wants me to do?" If you can answer those questions with a great big "YES," then go ahead. But if you're uncertain if the choice you are about to make is the right one, slow down. Why? Because that's what Solomon says . . . and that's what God says, too!

Wise choices bring you happiness; unwise choices don't. So whenever you have a choice to make, choose wisely.

WOW
Life is a series of choices between
the bad, the good, and the best.
Everything depends on how we choose.
Vance Havner

Some choices are up to the parents: Certainly, we want to give our children the chance to make decisions on their own, but some decisions must be reserved for the wisest men and women of the family (responsible parents like you). When it comes to the health, well-being, and safety of your child, you must decide.

63

Dear Lord,
help me to make choices that
are pleasing to You. Help me
to be honest, patient, and kind.
And above all, help me to follow
the teachings of Jesus,
not just today, but every day.

Amen

13

Let's Be Thankful!

It is good to give thanks to the LORD,
to sing praises to the Most High.
It is good to proclaim your unfailing love
in the morning, your faithfulness
in the evening.

৯ ৯ ৯

Psalm 92:1-2 NLT

Do you have a thankful attitude? Hopefully so! After all, you've got plenty of things to be thankful for. Even during those times when you're angry or tired, you're a very lucky person.

Who has given you all the blessings you enjoy? Your parents are responsible, of course. But all of your blessings really start with God. That's why you should say "Thank You" to God many times each day. He's given you so much . . . so thank Him, starting now.

Two magic words: Thank you! Your parents will never get tired of hearing those two little words, and neither will your friends. And neither, for that matter, will God.

WOW
Thanksgiving is good
but Thanksliving is better.
Jim Gallery

You can't count all your blessings . . . they're simply too many of them. But, as a Christian parent, you know where to start counting: Your Heavenly Father, His only Son, and your own children.

Dear Lord,
You have given me so many
blessings, and You want to
give me even more. Thank You.
Here's how I will show
my thanks: I will have a good
attitude, I will be kind to other
people, and I will behave myself.

Amen

14

Blaming Others . . .

. . . each will receive his own reward according to his own labor.

🌀 🌀 🌀

1 Corinthians 3:8 HCSB

When something goes wrong, do you look for somebody to blame? And do you try to blame other people even if you're the one who made the mistake? Hopefully not!

It's silly to try to blame other people for your own mistakes, so don't do it.

If you've done something you're ashamed of, don't look for somebody to blame; look for a way to say, "I'm sorry, and I won't make that same mistake again."

Blaming others is easy . . . but it's usually wrong. Fixing mistakes is harder . . . but it's usually right.

WOW
You'll never win the blame game,
so why even bother to play?
Marie T. Freeman

Blaming others is easy, Part II . . . It's easy (and quite natural) for your child to find fault in others and spread blame to others. That's why it's up to you, as the parent, to teach your child to take responsibility . . . and to learn from his mistakes!

Dear Lord,
when I make a mistake,
I want to admit it. Help me not
to blame others for the mistakes
that I make. And when
I make a mistake,
help me to learn from it.

Amen

15

You Can Do It . . .
If You
Stick to It!

We must not become tired of doing good.

🌀🌀🌀

Galatians 6:2 ICB

If you think you can do something, then you can probably do it. If you think you can't do something, then you probably won't do it.

So remember this: if you're having a little trouble getting something done, don't get mad, don't get frustrated, don't get discouraged, and don't give up. Just keep trying . . . and believe in yourself.

When you try hard—and keep trying hard—you can really do amazing things . . . but if you quit at the first sign of trouble, you'll miss out. So here's a good rule to follow: when you have something that you want to finish, finish it . . . and finish it sooner rather than later.

If things don't work out at first, don't quit. If you never try, you'll never know how good you can be.

WOW
By perseverance,
the snail reached the ark.
C. H. Spurgeon

Parent Tip

Remember the advice of Winston Churchill: He said, "Never give in; never give in; never give in." And that's good advice whether you're leading a nation or a family.

Dear Lord,
when I want to give up,
help me remember how
important it is to keep trying.
And when I'm worried or upset,
help me remember to talk to
my parents and to You.

Amen

16

Telling the Truth

The honest person will live safely,
but the one who is dishonest
will be caught.

೫ ೫ ೫

Proverbs 10:9 ICB

What is your attitude about telling the truth? Should you be honest with your parents? Certainly. With your brothers and sisters? Of course. With cousins, grandparents, aunts, and uncles? Yes! In fact, you should be honest with everybody in your family because honesty starts at home.

If you can't be honest in your own house, how can you expect to be honest in other places, like at church or at school? So make sure that you're completely honest with your family. If you are, then you're much more likely to be honest with everybody else.

It's better to say nothing: If you're tempted to say something that isn't true, don't say anything. A closed mouth tells no lies.

WOW
God doesn't expect you to be perfect, but he does insist on complete honesty.

Rick Warren

Discuss the importance of honesty: Teach the importance of honesty every day, and, if necessary, use words.

Dear Lord,
sometimes it's hard to tell
the truth. But even when
telling the truth isn't easy,
it's the right thing to do. So,
I'll do my best to tell the truth—
even when it's hard. When I tell
the truth, I'll be glad I did,
my friends and parents will be
glad I did, and You, dear God,
will be glad I did, too.

Amen

17
Respecting Other People

Show respect for all people.
Love the brothers and sisters
of God's family.

§ § §

1 Peter 2:17 ICB

Do you try to have a respectful attitude toward everybody? Hopefully so!

Should you be respectful of grown-ups? Of course. Teachers? Certainly. Family members? Yes. Friends? Yep, but it doesn't stop there. The Bible teaches us to treat all people with respect.

Respect for others is habit-forming: the more you do it, the easier it becomes. So start practicing right now. Say lots of kind words and do lots of kind things, because when it comes to kindness and respect, practice makes perfect.

Everybody is a VIP: VIP means "Very Important Person." To God, everybody is a VIP, and you should treat every person with dignity, patience, and respect.

WOW
If you will honor a person out of respect for God, you can be assured that God will honor you.
Beth Moore

Respect for all people: Children may seek to find humor in the misfortunes of others; children may, on occasion, exhibit cruelty toward other children. Be watchful for such behaviors and correct them with enthusiasm and vigor.

83

Dear Lord,
let me remember to be
respectful and kind to
everybody, starting with
my family and friends.
And, let me share the love
that I feel in my heart
with them . . . and with You!

Amen

18

It Starts in the Heart

God has chosen you . . . . He loves you.
So always do these things:
Show mercy to others, be kind, humble,
gentle, and patient.

🌀 🌀 🌀

Colossians 3:12 NCV

An attitude of kindness starts in your heart and works its way out from there.

Do you listen to your heart when it tells you to be kind to other people? Hopefully, you do. After all, lots of people in the world aren't as fortunate as you are—and some of these folks are living very near you.

Ask your parents to help you find ways to do nice things for other people. And don't forget that everybody needs love, kindness, and respect, so you should always be ready to share those things, too.

Keep your eyes open for somebody to help:
Someone very near you may need a helping hand or a kind word, so keep your eyes
open, and look for people who need your help,
whether at home, at church, or at school.

WOW
Our Lord was very patient—
and very compassionate.
Vance Havner

Parent Tip

It's good to feel compassion for others
. . . but it's better to do something to
ease their suffering. Martin Luther wrote,
"Faith never asks whether good works are
to be done, but has done them before there
is time to ask the question, and it is always
doing them." So when in doubt, do something
good for somebody. That's how you'll teach
your child the art and the joys of compassionate Christianity.

87

Dear Lord,
let me help others in every way
that I can. Jesus served
others; I can, too. I will serve
other people with my good deeds
and with my prayers. And I will
give thanks for everybody
who helps me.

Amen

19
Watch What You Think

Fix your thoughts on what is true and honorable and right. Think about things that are pure and lovely and admirable. Think about things that are excellent and worthy of praise.

෯ ෯ ෯

Philippians 4:8 NLT

Do you try to think the kind of thoughts that make you happy, not sad? The Bible says that you should.

Do you try to think about things that are true and right? The Bible says that you should.

Do you turn away from bad thoughts—and away from people who misbehave? The Bible says that you should.

The Bible instructs you to guard your thoughts against things that are hurtful or wrong. So remember this: when you turn away from the bad thoughts and bad people, you've made a very wise choice.

KiD TiP

Good thoughts create good deeds. Good thoughts lead to good deeds and bad thoughts lead elsewhere. So guard your thoughts accordingly.

WOW

The things we think are the things that feed our souls. If we think on pure and lovely things, we shall grow pure and lovely like them; and the opposite is also true.

Hannah Whitall Smith

Parent Tip

Be positive: If your thoughts tend toward the negative end of the spectrum, redirect them. How? You can start by counting your blessings and by thanking your Father in heaven. And while you're at it, train yourself to begin thinking thoughts that are more rational, more accepting, and more upbeat (Philippians 4:8) . . . for your children's sake.

Dear Lord,
help me think about things that
are good, things that are true,
and things that are right . . .
starting right now!

Amen

20

Words Are Important

Pleasant words are like a honeycomb.
They make a person happy and healthy.

෴ ෴ ෴

Proverbs 16:24 ICB

Do you like for people to say nice words to you? Yes, you do! And that's exactly how other people feel, too. That's why it's important to say things that make people feel better, not worse.

Your words can make other people feel better . . . or not. Make certain that you're the kind of person who says helpful things, not hurtful things. And, make sure that you're the kind of person who helps other people feel good about themselves.

Remember: everybody needs to hear kind words, and that's exactly the kind of words they should hear from you!

If you can't think of a nice thing to say . . . please keep quiet. It's better to say nothing than to hurt someone's feelings.

WOW
Fill the heart with the love of Christ
so that only truth and purity
can come out of the mouth.
Warren Wiersbe

Words matter. The words you speak will help shape the kids you love . . . and once you speak those words, you cannot "un-speak" them. Even if you're not speaking directly to your kids, you can be sure that your kids are listening, so choose your words carefully.

Dear Lord,
I want the things that I say
to be pleasing to you.
Help me remember to be
a kind person, and help me
say things that make the world—
and my heart—a better place.

Amen

21

Choosing
Friends Wisely

A friend loves you all the time.

ട ട ട

Proverbs 17:17 ICB

If your friends misbehave, do you misbehave right along with them, or do you tell them to stop? Usually, it's much easier to go along with your friends, even if you know they're misbehaving. But it's always better to do the right thing, even if it's hard.

Sometimes, grown-ups must stand up for the things they believe in. When they do, it can be hard for them, too. But the Bible tells us over and over again that we should do the right thing, not the easy thing.

When your friends misbehave, it can spoil everything. So if your friends behave badly, don't copy them! And if your friends keep behaving badly, choose different friends.

If you want to make new friends, how can you do it? A good way to make friends—and a good way to keep them—is to become a better listener. Most people are happy to tell you about themselves, and they'll be even happier if you listen carefully. So learn to be a good listener—it's a good way to make new friends.

WOW
The best times in life are made even better when shared with a dear friend.
Luci Swindoll

Parent Tip

Help from the sidelines: As parents, we can't make friendships for our children, but we can coach them on the art of making friends. All of us, whether youngsters or grown-ups, make friends by treating others as we wish to be treated. And if that sounds suspiciously like the Golden Rule, that's because it is the Golden Rule.

99

Dear Lord,
other people may want me
to misbehave, but You want me
to behave myself. And that's
what I want, too—I want to do
what's right. So help me do
the right thing, Lord,
even when it's hard.

Amen

22

What the Bible Says

Your word is like a lamp for my feet
and a light for my way.

🌀 🌀 🌀

Psalm 119:105 ICB

The Bible is God's message to you, and He wants you to read it. If you and your parents read the Bible every day, you'll be reminded of God's rules, God's love, and God's Son Jesus.

Since the Bible is important to God, it should be important to you, too. In fact, the Bible is the most important book you'll ever own. It's God's Holy Word. Read it every day, and follow its instructions. If you do, you'll be glad you did . . . and so will God.

Try it, you'll like it! Give the Bible a try . . . the more you learn from it, the more you'll want to learn.

WOW
The surest, most productive,
and most effective way to receive
God's guidance is the Bible.
Bill Hybels

Children's Bible? Take a close look. If your child doesn't already own one, consider purchasing a translation of the Holy Bible specifically intended for children. These translations are amazingly helpful because of their simplicity and clarity.

Dear Lord,
the Bible is Your gift to me.
Let me use it, let me trust it,
and let me obey it, today
and every day that I live.

Amen

23

No More Tantrums

Don't become angry quickly,
because getting angry is foolish.

🌀 🌀 🌀

Ecclesiastes 7:9 NCV

Temper tantrums are so silly. And so is pouting. So, of course, is whining. When we lose our tempers, we say things that we shouldn't say, and we do things that we shouldn't do. Too bad!

The Bible tells us that it is foolish to become angry and that it is wise to remain calm. That's why we should learn to control our tempers before our tempers control us.

Time out! If you become angry, the time to step away from the situation is before you say unkind words or do unkind things—not after. It's perfectly okay to place yourself in "time out" until you can calm down.

WOW
When you strike out in anger,
you may miss the other person,
but you will always hit yourself.
Jim Gallery

If you can control your anger, you'll help them see the wisdom in controlling theirs.

Dear Lord,
help me to keep away from angry
thoughts and angry people.
And if I am tempted to have
a temper tantrum, help me
to calm down before I do.

Amen

24

The Decision to Do What's Right

The LORD has already told you what is good, and this is what he requires: to do what is right, to love mercy, and to walk humbly with your God.

෯ ෯ ෯

Micah 6:8 NLT

King Solomon gave us wonderful advice for living wisely. Solomon said that we should keep our eyes "focused on what is right." In other words, we should do our best to say and do the things that we know are pleasing to God.

The next time you're tempted to say an unkind word or to say something that isn't true, remember the advice of King Solomon. Solomon knew that it's always better to do the right thing, even when it's tempting to do otherwise. So if you know something is wrong, don't do it; instead, do what you know to be right. When you do, you'll be saving yourself a lot of trouble and you'll be obeying the Word of God.

No so fast! If you're about to do something, but you're not sure if it's the right thing to do, slow down! It's better to make a good decision than a fast decision.

WOW

If you lack knowledge, go to school.
If you lack wisdom, pray about it.

Vance Havner

Parent Tip

Helping your child make wise choices . . . it's not just important to teach your child what to think. It's also important to teach your child how to think (and there's a big difference between the two).

Dear Lord,
there's a right way to do things
and a wrong way. Help me to do
things the right way,
today and every day.

Amen

25

Don't Be Too Hard on Yourself

If you hide your sins, you will not succeed.
If you confess and reject them,
you will receive mercy.

�æ 〆 〆

Proverbs 28:13 NCV

When you make a mistake, do you get really mad at yourself . . . or maybe really, really, really mad? Hopefully not! After all, everybody makes mistakes, and nobody is expected to be perfect.

Even when you make mistakes, God loves you . . . so you should love yourself, too.

So the next time you make a mistake, learn from it. And after you've learned your lesson, try never to make that same mistake again. But don't be too hard on yourself. God doesn't expect you to be perfect, and since He loves you anyway, you should feel that way, too.

When you make a mistake, learn something . . . and forgive someone: yourself. Remember, you don't have to be perfect to be wonderful.

WOW
The happiest people in the world are
not those who have no problems,
but the people who have learned to live
with things that are less than perfect.

James Dobson

Parents aren't perfect, either: The perfect parent does not exist. So don't be too hard on yourself when you fall short of absolute perfection (or, for that matter, when you fall short of near-perfection). Do your best, and trust God with the rest.

Dear Lord,
when I ask for Your forgiveness,
You give it. When I make
mistakes, help me to learn
my lessons . . . and help me
to forgive myself.

Amen

26

Count Your Blessings . . . and Keep Counting!

I pray also that you will have greater understanding in your heart so you will know the hope to which he has called us and that you will know how rich and glorious are the blessings God has promised his holy people.

৯ ৯ ৯

Ephesians 1:18-19 NCV

If you sat down and began counting your blessings, how long would it take? A very, very long time! Your blessings include your life, your family, your friends, your talents, and your possessions, for starters. But, your greatest blessing—a gift that is yours for the asking—is God's gift of eternal life through Christ Jesus.

You can never count up every single blessing that God has given you, but it doesn't hurt to try . . . so get ready, get set, go—start counting your blessings RIGHT NOW!

Want to cheer yourself up? Count your blessings. If you need a little cheering up, start counting your blessings . . . and keep counting until you feel better.

WOW

We do not need to beg God to bless us;
He simply cannot help it.

Hannah Whitall Smith

Help your kid count . . . their blessings!
We live in a prosperous society where children may take many of their blessings for granted. Your job, as a responsible parent, is to help your child understand how richly they have been blessed.

Dear Lord,
today I will begin counting
my blessings . . .
and I will keep counting them
every day of my life.

Amen

27
Looking for the Good Things

Summing it all up, friends, I'd say you'll do
best by filling your minds and meditating
on things true, noble, reputable,
authentic, compelling, gracious—
the best, not the worst . . . .

֍ ֍ ֍

Philippians 4:8 MSG

If you look for the good in other people, you'll probably find it. And, if you look for the good things in life, you'll probably find them, too.

But if spend your time looking for things that aren't so good, you'll most certainly find plenty of bad things to look at. So what should you do? It's simple: you should look for the good things, of course.

When you start looking for good things, you'll find them everywhere: in church, at school, in your neighborhood, and at home.

So don't waste your time on things that make you feel angry, discouraged, worried, guilty, or afraid. Look, instead, for the good things in life, the things that God wants you to pay attention to. You'll be glad you did . . . and God will be glad, too.

Before you watch anything on television . . . ask your parents if it's okay.

WOW
What you see is what you become.

Marie T. Freeman

What should you allow them to watch on TV? Before you decide which programs are appropriate for your child, ask yourself this question: Does God approve?

Dear Lord,
let my words and my deeds
be good. Let me praise You,
Father, by following in
the footsteps of Your Son,
and let others see Him
through me.

Amen

28

Excuses, Excuses, Excuses . . .

You, therefore, have no excuse,
you who pass judgment on someone else,
for at whatever point you judge the other,
you are condemning yourself.

க க க

Romans 2:1 NIV

What is an excuse? Well, when you make up an excuse, that means that you try to come up with a good reason that you didn't do something that you should have done.

Anybody can make up excuses, and you can, too. But you shouldn't get into the habit of making too many excuses. Why? Because excuses don't work. And why don't they work? Because everybody has already heard so many excuses that almost everybody can recognize excuses when they hear them.

So the next time you're tempted to make up an excuse, don't. Instead of making an excuse, do what you think is right. After all, the very best excuse of all . . . is no excuse.

The habit of making excuses is a bad habit. Excuses lead to trouble. If you're in the habit of making excuses, the best day to stop that habit is today.

WOW

We need to stop giving out excuses and start looking at and listening to Jesus.

Anne Graham Lotz

Excuses, excuses, excuses: As parents of young children, we hear lots and lots of excuses, some of which are valid, but many of which are not. It's our job to determine the difference between valid excuses and imaginary ones, and then to help our children understand the difference between the two.

Dear Lord,
help me to do the right thing
when it needs to be done . . .
so that I won't need
to make excuses.

Amen

A Happy Heart...
Day by Day

Create in me a pure heart, God,
and make my spirit right again.

ᔕ ᔕ ᔕ

Psalm 51:10 NCV

If we could decide to be happy "once and for all," life would be so much simpler, but it doesn't seem to work that way. If we want happiness to last, we need to create good thoughts every day that we live. Yesterday's good thoughts don't count . . . we've got to think more good thoughts today.

Each new day is a gift from God, so treat it that way. Think about it like this: today is another wonderful chance to celebrate God's gifts.

So celebrate—starting now—and keep celebrating forever!

A happy heart every day: Remember: You can choose to have a good attitude or a not-so-good attitude. And it's a choice you make every day.

WOW

If you want to be truly happy, you won't find it on an endless quest for more stuff. You'll find it in receiving God's generosity and in passing that generosity along.

Bill Hybels

A positive attitude is contagious . . . your children can catch it from you . . . and they should!

Dear Lord,
help me have an attitude that is
pleasing to You as I count
my blessings today, tomorrow,
and every day.

Amen

30

Let's Praise God!

Great is the LORD!
He is most worthy of praise!

♫ ♫ ♫

Psalm 145:3 NLT

The Bible makes it clear: it pays to say "thank You" to God. But sometimes, we may not feel like thanking anybody, not even our Father in heaven.

If we ever stop praising God, it's a big mistake . . . a VERY BIG mistake.

When you stop to think about it, God has been very generous with you . . . and He deserves a great big "thanks" for all those amazing gifts.

Do you want an attitude that pleases God? Then make sure that your attitude praises God. And don't just praise Him on Sunday morning. Praise Him every day, starting with this one.

Praise Him! One of the reasons you go to church is to praise God. But, you need not wait until Sunday rolls around to thank your Heavenly Father. Instead, you can praise Him many times each day by saying silent prayers that only He can hear.

WOW

The time for praise is now.
Let us begin to do our part now.
Hannah Whitall Smith

Parent Tip

Think about His blessings: Today, as you hug your child or kiss your spouse—or as you gaze upon a passing cloud or marvel at a glorious sunset—think of what God has done for you and yours. And, everytime you notice a gift from the Giver of all things good, praise Him. His works are marvelous, His gifts are beyond understanding, and His love endures forever.

135

Dear Lord,
today I will thank You for
all Your blessings. And I'll do
the same thing tomorrow,
and every day after that.
You never stop loving me,
and I will never stop
praising You.

Amen

31

Jesus Loves Me, This I Know

And I am convinced that nothing can ever separate us from his love. Whether we are high above the sky or in the deepest ocean, nothing in all creation will ever be able to separate us from the love of God that is revealed in Christ Jesus our Lord.

৯ ৯ ৯

Romans 8:38–39 NLT

Perhaps you've heard these words before: "Jesus loves me, this I know, for the Bible tells me so." Of course, these words can be found in the song "Jesus Loves Me." It's a wonderful song that should remind you of something very important: Jesus loves you very much.

When you invite Jesus to become your friend, He will do it . . . and He'll be your friend forever. If you make mistakes, He'll still be your friend. If you misbehave, He'll still love you. If you feel sorry or sad, He can help you feel better.

Yes, Jesus loves you more than you know. And when you welcome Him into your heart, you will be blessed now and forever.

What a friend you have in Jesus: Jesus loves you, and He offers you eternal life with Him in heaven. Invite Him into your heart. Now!

WOW

Jesus is the purest gold;
He is light without darkness;
He is altogether lovely.

C. H. Spurgeon

Parent Tip

Jesus loves you, this you know . . . and your children should know this, too! Of course you know that Jesus loves you. But it's up to you to make sure that they know that you know. So remind them often.

Dear Lord,
I know that You love me today
and that You will love me
forever. And I thank You for
Your love . . . today and forever.

Amen

Bible Verses
to Memorize

For God so loved the world
that he gave his only Son,
so that everyone who
believes in him will not
perish but have eternal life.

John 3:16 NLT

Anything is possible
if a person believes.

Mark 9:23 NLT

But happy are those . . .
whose hope is in
the LORD their God.

Psalm 146:5 NLT

Be still,
and know that I am God . . . .
Psalm 46:10 KJV

Choose for yourselves this
day whom you will serve . . .
as for me and my household,
we will serve the LORD.

Joshua 24:15 NIV

My purpose is to give life
in all its fullness.

John 10:10 HCSB

Are any among you suffering?
They should keep on praying
about it.

James 5:13 NLT

Ask and it will be given to you;
seek and you will find;
knock and the door will be
opened to you. For everyone
who asks receives; he who seeks
finds; and to him who knocks,
the door will be opened.

Matthew 7:7-8 NIV

Foolish people are always
getting into quarrels,
but avoiding quarrels will
bring you honor.
Proverbs 20:3 ICB

A person who does not quickly
get angry shows that he has
understanding. But a person who
quickly loses his temper
shows his foolishness.

Proverbs 14:29 ICB

And yet the reason you don't have what you want is that you don't ask God for it.

James 4:2 NLT

Be an example to the believers
in word, in conduct, in love,
in spirit, in faith, in purity.

1 Timothy 4:12 NKJV

Jesus replied, "I assure you:
Unless someone is born again,
he cannot see
the kingdom of God."
John 3:3 HCSB

The L<small>ORD</small> bless you and keep you;
The L<small>ORD</small> make His face
shine upon you,
and be gracious to you.

Numbers 6:24-25 NKJV

But grow in grace,
and in the knowledge of our Lord
and Saviour Jesus Christ . . . .

2 Peter 3:18 KJV

All things are possible for
the one who believes.

Mark 9:23 NCV

Little Book Devotions help parents and children discuss important Biblical themes by relating those themes to the challenges of everyday life. These books are intended to be read *by* parents *to* children. Current titles include:

Little Book Devotions Honesty
Little Book Devotions Kindness
Little Book Devotions Patience
Little Book Devotions Forgiveness
Little Book Devotions Self-Control
Little Book Devotions Sharing
Little Book Devotions Obedience
Little Book Devotions Self-Esteem

Additional titles are coming soon.

Little Book Devotions are available in LifeWay Christian Stores.